OVER
EXPOSED

D0813369

OVER EXPOSED

a poetic memoir

Terri Muuss

JB Stillwater Publishing Company
Albuquerque, New Mexico

Copyright © 2013 Terri Muuss, all rights reserved.

No portion of this publication may be reproduced, stored in a retrieval system, or transmitted in any form or by any means, electronic, mechanical, photocopying, recording, or otherwise without the prior written permission of Terri Muuss, unless such copying is expressly permitted by federal copyright law. Address inquiries to Permissions, JB Stillwater Publishing Company, 12901 Bryce Avenue NE, Albuquerque, NM 87112.

Library of Congress Cataloging-in-Publication Data
Muuss, Terri.
  Over exposed : a poetic memoir / Terri Muuss.
    pages cm
  ISBN 978-1-937240-23-3 (pbk.) -- ISBN 978-1-937240-24-0 (epub)
  I. Title.
  PS3613.U87O94 2013
  811'.6--dc23
                                    2013007717

JB Stillwater Publishing Company
12901 Bryce Avenue, NE
Albuquerque, NM 87112
http://www.jbstillwater.com
20130408
Printed in the United States of America

Author's Note: This book is based on my experiences over a four decade period. It is told as accurately as possible given the constraints of memory and time. Some names and identifying details have been changed, some characters and events compressed.

To Matt—for Lincoln Center fountains
and shoes that fit

CONTENTS

FOREWORD

If you bring forth what is in you, what you bring forth will save you. If you do not bring forth what is within you, what you do not bring forth will destroy you.

(Gnostic) Gospel of St. Thomas

I remember the first time I saw Terri Muuss perform her one-woman show, *Anatomy of a Doll*. Wherever she moved on stage, there was a light, not just *on* her, but *in* her. She'd written the performance pieces as poems over a number of years, in workshops I'd led. Over those years, as her work came to light, literally, it felt as if I were looking into a deep green pool, as each piece would rise, sink, rise again.

I say this because the fact of this book at all is extraordinary. These poems will take you into the artery of memory, memory in fact that comes not as a seamless whole, but in fragments, in off-center snapshots. Why?

Because Terri Muuss is speaking of the un speak able. She is speaking of trauma. But do not turn away. For out of that harsh crucible, she has come to affirm, she has come to show what poetry can do.

i

In the landmark book, *Trauma and Recovery,* Judith
Herman, MD, delineates the dialectic for those who
have experienced trauma: "The will to deny – the will
to proclaim is the dialectic of psychological trauma."
We have all perhaps read folktales about ghosts who
refuse to rest in their graves until their stories are
told. There is wisdom in this.

As we enter into yet another year of war(s) abroad,
and soldiers come home, we see the effects of trauma;
we see it in the streets, in the hospitals, the jails, and
in the homeless. Post Traumatic Stress Disorder. By
now we have learned its initials. But also we see *art*
being made out of the madness: Brian Turner, Bruce
Weigl, Yusef Komunyakaa, among others.

My own poetry book, *Vocabulary of Silence,* written
from the viewpoint of a Witness-From-Afar to the
continued US wars in Iraq and Afghanistan and the
fact of Abu Ghraib, expresses in poems the failure of
language, and, the need for language.

In the pages that follow, Muuss brings us close to
what we might describe as the secret war, the
intimate war, which resides in closed rooms, in

seemingly ordinary homes. Yet these poems are written, reader, with such delicacy, such concern for image, for pause, and purpose—for, in fact, beauty.

Yes, these poems and prose pieces turn on the beauty of poetry, of what art can accomplish. I bid you open the book. It is a miracle.

Veronica Golos
Taos, New Mexico, 2013

...because truly being here is so much; because everything here apparently needs us, this fleeting world, which in some strange way keeps calling to us. Us, the most fleeting of all.

Rainer Maria Rilke

PROLOGUE: PANORAMA

The olive green jacket
arrived with my father
inside. The years had
made him smaller
and he held his head

tilted forward as if
the weight of living had finally
impelled him to angle
in. He was taking me

to the bank of a
coffee-colored lake
to watch duck
heads disappear,
catching small things

below the surface
with sharpened beaks.
Before we spoke,
he took the plain

silver watch out
of his pocket, held it
briefly to his ear then
wound it three times
with swift flicks

of thumb and forefinger.
The unsaid pressed down
from the indigo
sky and behind me—

behind me the new-
leafed trees swayed.
When he spoke
his voice scraped—
a wheat reed

brushing the palm
of my hand.

SHUTTER

My past washes back, a low tide, a haunting song.

Veronica Golos

MEMORIES COME

light through a prism   the story refracted   spaces

                between the lines   white spaces on the
canvas
of color   a shuffled deck of cards   52 pickup
they land   patterned
                        random   disjointed
shuffled   ordered
                chaotic   missing parts   under the sofa
behind the bookcase   under

the rug   a thread   pulling   inching me

                                                forward.

WILD VIOLETS

My father's hand tight around a fistful of pennies. They shine like mirrors as he counts them out on the edge of my Holly Hobby bedspread at midnight. *One, two, three, four...* I am paralyzed watching him. I am waiting. I want those pennies but what must I do to have them? They are painfully new, reflectively shiny. They dazzle me. I know how cold they will be until warmed in the tiny palm of my hand. They are such a precious thing. I want to put the pennies in my mouth. In the sides of my mouth, those copper pennies will taste like blood. He gathers me onto his lap and strokes my knee. In my right hand is a folded picture from one of my father's hunting and fishing magazines. I like to look at the pictures of the fish: their glassy eyes tinged with blood, their clipped fins. I stare for hours at the huge fingers which push themselves under the fishes' vermillion gills as they are held aloft into the white air. Their gills are red, so bright, held by men with yellow, crooked teeth and dark smiles. As I tighten my grip on the wrinkled paper in my hand, my father begins to smile, too.

Later, I escape outside and stoop to collect violets and put them in the white wicker of my bicycle basket. I carefully pick each one at its base and kiss its delicate head before bundling them with bits of string or paperclips. I ride for long hours up and down Ellen Street, leaving small gifts of freshly picked dandelions and violets in my neighbors' mailboxes. I ride my bike until my Achilles ache and the sun drips down the sky, leaving a wash of watercolor. "Red sky at night, sailors delight. Red sky in the morning, sailors take warning," I pronounce to the sky. At dusk, I go into the open field on our street to lie down in the tall grass and listen to the crickets sing until the streetlights come on. Most days, I run home so as not to be late. But some evenings, I lie for a few extra moments and allow myself to fade into the backdrop of night: to be lost, invisible, and yet a part of something larger. Soon, I hear my mother's call summoning me back to our house, the one with the peeling paint and secrets. Returning to my bike, I find the dry carcasses of violets wilted into the cracks of my white wicker bicycle basket.

FLASHBACK: CORNER OF 183rd STREET

syrupy brown insides
of whiskey bottles
a tan recliner
small animal bones
a single gray feather buried
in a dead patch of pine forest.
A cavern of longing—

how beneath my pillow
I pressed my cassette player
to my ear: *Sweet Dreams*
played over and over; a cat
howled under the streetlight.

Still as nails,
blood red as my mother's
tossed leather purse,

I stop
at the corner, wait—
long pieces of straw in my throat,

wait—

for *it* to begin
again.

SCARLET LETTER

In fifth grade
my father's secrets
start to breed under my red
confirmation dress—
dig deep in the tunnel of my inner
ear, cling to sentry hairs
on the nape of my neck—

his secrets: black bodies,
glassy eyes, squeeze
beneath my fingernails—
quiet as eggs;
they spin a red thread
that cuts me inside
out.

SECOND GRADE

My daddy. My daddy is very tall.

He is a police man. He carries a gun. He lets me fire the gun. He holds me up high. Up and up and then I pull the trigger. I don't tell him, but I don't like it much. The sound is so loud, it's scary. At work they call my daddy the Big Man.

Or Frac. His partner's name is Fric. My daddy collects things. He collects beer steins from Germany, patches from different police departments, and matchbooks from all over the world.

My daddy and I are best friends. We go on walks every night after dinner where he tells me secret things. Secret things.

My daddy is a veteran. That means he fought in a war.

Well, he says they didn't call it a war in Panama. But he says he still lost his hearing in one ear, whether it was a war or not.

He got to wear a beret in this war. And dog tags.

I don't know why they call them that.

My daddy loves me so much. He pulls me into his
arms. My daddy is so strong. Pulls me into his arms,
tighter, tighter and I just dis   disss   disappear. I
disappear.

SUNDAY MORNING BLUE

yellow balloon floats
up, up, sky a giant
blue mouth—my foot
this is my foot
my foot
and a big yellow
balloon floating up.
lying in my stroller, shade
from my white hat, kicking feet
kicking, kicking 'cause I can,
i kick and kick and watch
the balloon string dances—
this is fun
mommy's laugh.
mommy's singing.
mommy's peek a boo.
peek a boo.
i see you!
where are you?
i see you!
where are you?
there you are!
where's the mommy?
where's the mommy?
i can't find you now.
where's the mommy?
i can't
find you.
big hands grab
my feet—
feet in the air, grab
my heels. i am a circle

my knees in my eyes—is this a game?
big hands, daddy hands—where
is mommy?
where is the yellow balloon?
are these
still my feet? the sky's
a mouth,
a red slash—peek a boo—

FATHER'S SECRET DRAWER

smells of ashes and sweat
and is cut in two by a black
cloth liner. On top: a gold
pen, tie tacks, small bag
of dried cloves, a picture
of his mother and a lump
of chewed gum.

Beneath: the metal casings
of shotgun shells, four huge teeth
with roots, a segment
of my baby hair trapped
between pieces of
tape and an assortment of thick
thumbnail clippings. In my palm

they look like mini moons. My father
uses them to pick
bits of food from between his yellow
teeth. At night, they gleam—
a mouth of stars above me,
his fingernails smooth
as glass—they stroke

my skin, white as pork.

THE DATE

I'm meeting him at his house. I will wear my little
blue skirt, the cute floral top he bought me at the mall
(Daddy likes to see me in new clothes), and my
favorite pair of silver earrings. The silver earrings
Daddy brought me from Long Beach Island, in the
shape of a conch shell, the pair that he picked out just
for me. My stepmother usually picks out everything,
but these Daddy saw and said, "My baby has to have
them." The gentle slope of shell curls around the pink
lobe of each ear, holding on as if for dear life. I think
I'm crazy to be so happy.

It is wrong but I can't help feeling the thrill of slowly
stealing him away from her. This is the second *her*. Is
it my fault he likes me better? I know what he wants; I
know just what to do.

The first time it was much harder. Many more days I
let the guilt drape itself over me like the lead cape at
the x-ray table, almost suffocating me. After all, the
first *her* was my mother.

Now, it's someone new. Someone who tells my father, "She shouldn't wear those sneakers to school." Someone who looks at me from the side of her face. And I hate her. My stepmother thinks she knows so much. The bun tied tightly up, her no-makeup face, the lingering scent of Emeraulde, the perfume that Daddy picked out just for her. But, youth is on my side. Her eyes show crow's feet, and the lines around her mouth are beginning to sink down.

And me, I'm 13 today.

HUNTER

In the stagnant
morning he readied
himself, a man going
on a date. The precision of his
fatigues, how he sprayed
himself with the scent

of dark woods, and doubled then
triple-checked his packing. He courted
instinct in the blue light.

My father would ferret
out a small trembling—
even 30 miles south
of our home—

wait—
for a nose, tail, white
underbelly to betray
itself and dart towards
ruin. One tensed
finger and my father's
hand at its neck, palming
the slowing thrum. He'd hoist

the full weight of his authority
into the truck. Spark drained, he'd carry
its limpness back to us like
a treasure.

Mother was left
to skin, section and freeze
what lay before her.

Yesterday, I drove in the fog
of twilight around my street's final curve
when a dotted white line disappeared
beneath my tire. In the rearview, I saw it

twitch, fur dancing in the smoke
of engine and steam. I stepped
out of my car, aflood
with adrenaline, and
stared at the rabbit through the eyes

of my father. The night hummed—
then the gray before morning.

FROM ABOVE

He's coming. I look out of my bedroom window just in time to see our tan station wagon pull into the gravel of our driveway. The car leaves its red taillight behind like a stain. My heart begins revving; I feel sick. The engine is shut off and things heighten: kaleidoscope colors, adrenaline pulling all into a center point, edges, warping bed, table, desk, a tug of war, white static snow falling, my mind—reverb on a guitar. I hear a baby crying down the hallway—in my head, in my ear, a tunnel deep inside. Is it a neighbor's baby? Pick it up. It's deafening—a movie version of a baby crying on Dolby surround sound, then a banging, banging, banging—a headboard banging? A door banging open? The heat? It's just the heat coming up in my cold room. The pipes. The heat coming up, shaking the ground, a volcano—no, no, a hot spring with steam shaking the pipes. It's so cold. The heat coming up through the wooden slats of the floor, coming up—Shhhhhh—coming up. The Father coming up the stairs. The stairs. I can hear him stealing up. A poisonous gas floating up the staircase. Holding breath. I know exactly which stair. The fourth one. The fifth one creaks—the section of banister missing a pole. The eighth stair, I am so cold. I am shaking, shaking free from myself. I can see me, a movie actress, playing a part. I am playing a part below me. Shhhhhh—I am floating. Below, I can see me: cold and shaking. I know there is static in that girl down there, but not in me. I am split from her. Floating the way they say you do when you die, while he stands in the doorway. I watch me pretending until he comes in, he comes in, comes in the girl below me, me. He comes to me, the girl asleep, pretending. Then he stays with me. He stays in me.

INNER MONSOON

I'm still here. A Ziploc bag—sealed: my lips, my heart, my legs. Can't get into me. This tall building can't be leaped in any bound. I'm like the roaches they say will be here long after nuclear annihilation. I am still here. In your backyard. Turn around. I'm those dandelions you mow down. They come right back. I'm springing up on you—a cat huge and hungry. I'm a black cat. Don't you cross my path. I'll kill you—all smiles with my fingers crossed behind my back. My heart is frozen solid, a glacier. I. Am. Still. Here. I am in front of you. Right in front of your face. You have to take notice. But unlike a man, for whom everything sharp and pointed is a weapon, I'll kill you with my curves.

FOCUS

...Open the hurt locker
and see what there is of knives
and teeth.

Brian Turner

WHAT HEALS

There is no fixed truth
in this moment—only the hollow
clank of knowing between
your ribs, the ticking
clock, the bomb in your
stomach. Grasp the cold
shovel. In absence, the heart
breathes; the lungs beat.

THE SHOE

My eyes are on the tongue—
not looking—a black smudge
on the wall. I am
my father's shoe—
beat up, black patent
leather. Somewhere above me—
a shoe tossed against the
wall, my father removes his holster
like a student sharpening
his pencil—I cannot look—
lines on the ceiling—his worn-
out shoe. The sole is pulling
away as father presses—
ting-ting-ting—his
loose and floppy buckle against
his service revolver.

AT THE END

The guy with the Fender
stared right through me.
Rhythm and blues shot

from the speakers and I knew
I would take him home. The red
leaves of maples and brown needles
of pines fell somewhere outside.

Inside, my shoe
stuck to the tacky spills
and the smoke from burning
ashtrays singed my throat.

"Can I buy you a drink?"
the voice from the speakers
purred into my ear. Yes.
He could.

After this one, my
apartment seemed haunted.
It creaked and wind
rushed through me—

the hushed whispers
of children.

BETWEEN THE DARK AND THE DAYLIGHT

My brother ties
the red balloon to his
wrist until—
whoosh—
the wind hangs
it on a telephone
pole. From there
the balloon dots
the pink underbelly
of sunset and
streetlights
coming on.
Get in here right now!
We fumble
over father's yell—
hide behind
the lilac bush
near the tarred
logs of our
neighbor's fence.
The wind kisses
the edge of my
flowered shirt
lifts it for a
moment—my brother
kisses my cheek
For good luck.
And we go—
inside.

THE T-SHIRT

The t-shirt. Eggshell white, worn almost all the way through. In the summer you could see my eight year-old brother's tan through the transparency of overwashing. There was a hole under the left armpit, and a smaller but more jagged one at the neckline. The neck and arms were lined in blue material. They seemed, at the end of the shirt's life, the only visible parameters the shirt had left. The iron-on in the center was long faded by overuse, but I think, if memory serves, it said *Dukes of Hazzard* in orange, with the picture of that famous car outlined in black. There were yellowish sweat stains under the right armpit and a spaghetti sauce stain below and to the side of the faded iron-on, brown but nearly perfectly circular.

I still can't understand why this was my brother's favorite shirt. I only know that I, too, came to love that shirt. It was stability. It was the summer of '81: streetlights, kickball and Carvel. It was riding your bike, hiding in the bushes and walking Bandit the neighbor's dog to the 7-11. It was as if that shirt were my brother's tattoo, his semi-conscious way of keeping things status quo. And whatever our parents could do to us, they couldn't seem to keep Chris from wearing that shirt, day in, day out, night in, night out, always, for years.

I can't remember the day he got the shirt. Maybe because all of our clothes were hand-me-downs, brought to us by parental friends in large green garbage bags for us to sift through. It wasn't until the cotton gave way and softened, or until Chris had pulled it over his crouched-up knees seven thousand times, that it became special. It wasn't until the spaghetti sauce, the hours of kickball, and the sweat stains sweetened the shirt somehow, made it lived in, that my brother began his campaign. The Cal Ripken of t-shirt use, my brother kept his streak up until it literally fell off his body in tatters. "That's it. Give me the shirt... *Give* me the shirt." My mother took the shirt from Chris and put it underneath the kitchen sink with a dozen or so other rags.

My mother did use the shirt-turned-rag once. One night, she sat huddled in the corner of her bedroom, leaning against the little nightstand, the digital clock flashing twelve o'clock, twelve o'clock, twelve o'clock like the garish neon light at the local topless bar my father sat at. She sat, pulling the cord of the nightlight on again, off again, on again, off again, crying and laughing simultaneously. In her lap sat my father's service revolver: cocked, loaded and wrapped in my brother's favorite shirt.

IN A HOLE

Thump. Thump. Thump. Thump. The music is drilling a
hole into my chest. It runs through me, waves of
sound that bounce against my spine and move my
body without consulting my brain. Sweat is pouring
down my back. The music is so loud it hurts, but I
throw myself at it like a rubber ball. My arms are
elastic and I can't feel my face. My heart is pounding
in the same rhythm as the thump, thump, thump of
the dance floor. I just know it will explode and I don't
care. Music crashes into walls as I fall into someone's
arms I don't know. They slowly kiss me and I linger,
cradled in arms that seem to have me securely for an
instant. Gradually, I am brought back to standing, but
my heart continues beating so fast and so hard I feel it
is likely to rip itself out of my chest and fall onto the
floor. My head tells me I need something else to quell
the storm brewing in my body.

With effort, I make my way through the sea of bodies
to the bathroom. Everything is unusually sharp and
emphatic, as though I must remember it all for a test
later. As I stumble across the dance floor, I pass some
guy in tight black pants, with no shirt on and a red

feathered boa clinging to the sweat on his arms and back. He shakes his long black hair in time to the music and I watch as it becomes a smudge of black charcoal before me in the air. I am instantly soaked in his sweat. It hits my face like pin-pricks of ice.

In the bathroom, I gently push my way past drag queens in tottering heels and pretty boys in chains and leather to find my place at the sink. In the metal basin, I see the remnants of someone's sick along with a half-smoked cigarette, some ashes and a lipstick mark. Resting my arms at the edge of the filthy basin, I draw my eyes up to find a vacant-eyed, hollow-cheeked, pale version of myself in the mirror. My pupils are enormous and I see with fascination that they have blotted all the color from my irises. I scan for any trace of sea-foam green and find nothing but a circle, so shiny and reflective. I remark to anyone who might hear me that I have black beetles for eyes. I turn on the water and gently dab my cheeks and forehead, careful not to smudge what remains of my elaborate eye makeup. I take my hands, still wet with water, and drag them along the desert of my tongue. I am thirstier than I have ever been, but having spent the last of my cash on two tabs of X, have no more money for the $7 bottles of water they are selling at the bar. The owners here at Twilo are smart enough to know that no one comes here to drink their crappy, watered-down alcohol, so they overcharge us for bottled water, knowing how dehydrated the drugs we take will make us. I shrug, carefully tilt my head to the side and drink from the grimy spigot. The water has a metallic quality to it, like blood in my mouth, but I don't care. I need it. I stumble back from the sink in my pleather boots and search for an empty bathroom stall, but here there are no single user stalls. Clumps of legs huddle behind bathroom doors, their owners deep in the negotiation of shared drug use. I am about to leave when suddenly, from behind, an arm links with my own and a smiling face appears next to mine. It is Trevor. He is a friend of my friends. We came here together tonight en masse and his friend Charles is friends with my friend Dan. I know very little about him except he is an amazing dancer and, ironically, works as a drug counselor in his other life. He strokes the inside of my arm with a dreamy fascination until one of the overcrowded stalls opens and empties. He quickly tugs me into the stall with him and locks the door behind us.

"You are X-ing too hard, girl. Here, do a bump of K,"
he says as he places the tiny spoon under my nose.

I hold one nostril closed and use a quick intake of
breath to take my medicine. I feel the tiny burn of it
enter me and a slow buzzing sensation begins growing
in my mind, like the feel of vibrating dental
equipment in your mouth. I close my eyes and see
strange patterns and lines. I can't help but smile. Yes!
THIS is what I needed. How did he know?

"Thanks," I say and my mouth lingers a bit too long on
the S so that it sounds as though I am hissing like a
snake. After doing his own bump, Trevor and I exit
the bathroom, arms still linked, and suddenly it dawns
on me: I feel... happy. I have been chemically chasing
this feeling for months, perhaps years, and I smile
again to myself, knowing that I will follow this feeling
wherever I need to. The music sounds so amazing to
me now, time feels frozen and I think to myself that
this moment *feels* amazingly like clarity, that this is
what infinity must feel like. A newfound energy
controls me now, a calmer force. *This,* I say to myself,
I can manage. Ecstasy has only taken me so far and
now I know what I need to take me home. This

combination is perfect and offers relief from the faceless, addling voices in my head. But I will need more. This small feeling of happiness must be magnified. If one bump is good, then two will be better and I can exponentially grow my happiness in perpetuity. I lean into Trevor and ask him to sit with me on the large sofas off to the side of the dance floor. I don't want my supply of happiness to go off dancing somewhere without me.

"Sure, honey," he says and we look for a place on the crowded couches to sit. Already I feel the bitter drip of the K in the back of my throat and I sniff it back quickly, knowing I need more right away. We sit down and I do another bump. And then another. Then one more for good measure.

"Slow down, sweetie," Trevor drawls at me with dreamy eyes, "we have all night." I lean back into the crushed velvet sofa and run my hands along the underside of the loveseat and the perfect red fabric there. Yes, we have all night. And I am gone.

Sometime later, I awake from my trance, slightly sick and dizzy. I have no idea how long I have been lying here. With intense effort, I try to bring myself to sitting up, but it is no use. I can not move. The sickening thump thump thump of the music is back in the core of my chest and I think I must be having a heart attack. I realize suddenly, and with alarm, that someone's face is in my face. It is Dan. He is talking to me. Asking me if I am okay. Am I okay? His question travels slowly through the canal of my ear into my brain and once it is there and registered fully, I try to speak. In my brain the words echo, "I don't know, I don't know, I don't know," but nothing comes out. I try again to speak. The words in my head are physically unable to exit my mouth. I am mute. I can not move. There is something sickeningly familiar about this... I have been here before. This feeling of being gone, immoveable, of being lost. It is almost too much to bear. This is too familiar. I need to shake this off. I need to be able to *move*.

"You can't speak, can you," he smiles. "You are in a K-hole, darlin'."

In a hole. Yes, I am. I am lost and sick and I have no idea how long I have been here. I need to get out. Please, God, won't someone help me. I have fallen into holes before and I often worry that the fabric of my mind has such rips and tears that I will fall through one day and never be found. I have to get out of here. Please help me get out of here.

CLOSET

I've been bad again. I couldn't help it. And now I've
made her wear her angry face. She crouches down to
my three year-old height by placing her hands on her
knees and thrusting her hips back. Then, she slowly
pushes her face into mine. "You are a bad, bad girl,"
she hisses, "you know we don't cry when mommy
leaves. That makes Mrs. Jones feel so bad, bad, bad."
With that, she swiftly grabs me by the crook of my
elbow, throws me into the open hall closet and shuts
the door.

Every day, Mommy leaves me with 72 year-old Mrs.
Jones. She sticks me in the closet to stop me from
crying, which only makes me scream. Yelling keeps
me in the closet longer, so I try to collapse my voice
into dust, bury it deep like a seed in the center of my
sternum.

Inside—the choking smell of mothballs and mold, the
damp, penetrating air. I feel the sides of the walls for
their limits and pull back bits of plaster and chips of
paint in my blind searching hands, an army of coats
scratching wool fingers over my skin. The absolute

black—a void I fall into. So deep I fall until I stop knowing the difference between myself and the darkness.

PASSING

Crows fly in formation
toward solid steel:
the bridge, a flightless bird, clipped
chipped paint,
gray upon gray.
I am aware of taking up
space.

The winter sun stains
the edge
of these South Bronx projects,
an experiment in cloning
one brick wall
identical to another
like dutiful soldiers

at roll call. The last light
bounces
off vacant windows—an extravagance—
ceremony of iron and light. Time

stops, I hear my pulse—

shift my bag,
left shoulder to right,
leave the sun slipping
off the street signs.

FEEDING

I've decided to stop eating. I will cut back on everything. I will count every calorie. I will be freer, lighter, less visible.

Lately, I feel a bull's eye on me: on the street, the A train, in the fruit market. Men infect me with words, with smiles. Eyes snatch at breasts, tongues pin me to subway walls, mouths like a cold speculum pry open my inner ear. Their words pound, pound me, a worn head of drum. Voices divide and conquer, dividing me from myself—

No more. They will not be able to yell *great tits* if I no longer have any. Yes, I will disappear. I can control how many carrot sticks I eat. I will drink nothing but water, eat only three raisins a day. I will evaporate, dissolve, implode, contract, shrink the sickness, kill the depravity in me. I will starve—it—to death.

COMFORT FOOD

for Helen Muuss

Burgundy roses drift
down the walls in brown slants
across the room. The tip
of my pink high-heeled shoe—
a sleeping dog at my feet.

At the square
kitchen table, I sit with my mother
stones in our mouths,
father spread out before us—
that forbidden meal.

The table is set:
spoon, fork, a knife sharp enough to
carve his initials into my arm.
"For you," mother says and
hands me a postcard—
a recent trip through the hills of North Carolina.

I imagine us there:
the roadside stands,
buying thick blackberries
in green cardboard containers,
the kitschy danger
of cheap motels, greasy
truck stops, homemade
cherry cobbler, mashed potatoes
gobs of butter—the gentle opening
of conversation.

We could put a thousand miles
between us and our
history.

I push back my chair from the table.
The legs grate against the linoleum,
a squawk from a falling bird.

VOICES/LITANY #1

Where was your mother? What happened to your
brother? Why didn't your mother protect you? Didn't
she know? How could she not know? How many
times did it happen? Where did it happen? How did
you feel? What do you mean you *disappeared*? What do
you mean you didn't know what was happening? How
can you not remember for years? How could you *not*
remember? Where was your mother? Did anyone else
in the family know? How did he hide it? Did he do this
to other girls? How do you know? Did it hurt? Was it
penetration or did he just touch you? What do you
mean by *grooming*? What's *grooming*? How could your
mother not know? Did your brother know it was
happening? Did you talk to anyone about it? Did
anyone at school notice? Were you afraid that other
people could tell? Did you lose sleep at night? Did you
have nightmares? Did you ask him to stop? Did you
say no? Did you call out? Did you tell anyone? Where
was your mother? Where was your brother? How
could no one know? How, how, *how* could your
mother not know?

LATE

I am flying through the air. I can see in slow motion
the arc of flight my bike takes as it is hurled against
the garage door. I know with certainty I will soon be
lying in pieces next to it. I should have never been five
minutes late. I need to be punished. My father is
right.

Watching as my brother sits on Thomas, the turkey
we thought was our pet, my father telling Chris to
hold him still. The ax lifts, then the blood. I can see
the absence in my brother's face. I, too, do not live
behind my eyes. Blood, blood everywhere. I know for
a fact I am dying, but I don't mind. I reach between
my legs and bring my bloody hand up to my face. The
blood is so dark I can see myself in it. I know that
there is a reason I am bleeding but can't remember
what it is.

The robin's nest next to my bedroom window
contains three small blue stones. I count on seeing
them every day, waiting for them to become chicks.
One day, I open my window to find three dried, dead
chicks with ants eating their blue fixed eyes. I run to

tell my father and he tells me how I killed them with my watching. "The mother bird abandoned them. She thought you would hurt her and so she left the babies to die. That is what they do." That is what they do.

ELKINS, NH

Black fly season peaked
in June. My brother and I
would wade up to our thighs,
digging out fresh-
water clams with our toes. I feared
the murk under my feet.
In those silent
hours, we never talked
about the tiny spaces between
the wood slats of our childhood.
We were comfortable
with the sinking
our ankles made into rotting
sediment and the buzzing
of mosquitoes circling
our heads. We'd stoop down
to catch striders and wait
for the inevitable sting.

CLICK

... I say
do what you are going to do, and I will tell about it.

Sharon Olds

PIECES

I don't remember the first time and I am not sure I
remember the last—

was one of those last times you can't imagine as the
last, so you don't file it away with any specificity. The
first time—

is still elusive. Just when I think I can touch the hem,
it unravels in my hand

the coarse feel of a cheap bedspread, small cracks
running in parallel lines along the beige ceiling, steam
rising out of heating vents, a crushing weight on top
of my small frame, and the breathlessness—

tiny pieces in a house that is not mine.

NEIGHBOR

One bead of sweat rolls down the nape of my neck to the middle of my back, where it settles into me. And I'm stuck. I can't move forward. My heart kicks against my temples, it wants out. There's a door at the top of the stairs, and a handle, I must open the door. My heart knocking against the cavity of my chest, knocking against my chest, knocking at the door, I must open the door. *Open the door, he's waiting for you to be a good girl* and I open the door, I open the door, I open the door to this old man from next door who brought gifts and would kiss my round, eight year-old face with a slight turn of his head and his hand firmly behind my head. My mother somehow vanished—*Now be a good girl*—leaving me with this man 60 years my elder, his rough face tearing up my skin; I think it must be bleeding or on fire. I must spit. I must run. I need to brush my teeth.

SIXTEEN, GOING DOWN

Dark purple
hit me

halfway through the concert.
Smoking pot, I thought

I was dissolving.
Air filled with chlorine,

a catch in the cloth
of my throat.

The lightheaded sedation
of bottomless waves.

Behind a tower of amps,
a door opened

in my mind. A supply
cabinet of empty

elevators. I'd have to travel
so much further

to get to the lighthouse, the redheads,
the white trellis, and the eyes

that recognize me.
I had so much further

still to drop.

BASEMENT PARTY, BROOKLYN

Hot steel shots of alcohol
burn every inch of me. The wagging
tongues of boys rasp like

sandpaper as the house
hulas in sensual circles, a striptease.
Gunpowder laced

candy corn, the wax
in lava lamps. "She's going
down," a boy laughs. My body's
erector

set crumbles against
invisible panes of glass. Inside,
the mannequins slow dance

as though time
is all they have.

LIFE OF THE PARTY

Daddy has big groups of people over, either his PBA buddies or just some friends late at night—they are fat white men sitting around telling dirty jokes, drinking, smoking, and being loud. Mom and Chris go to sleep. I am slowly moving downstairs at my daddy's request, two feet on a step, two feet on a step, over and over—carefully, so as not to slip down the uncarpeted staircase in footie pajamas—coming down to entertain the men. It's late and everyone else is sleeping, but I am special and use that special when I kiss each one of them on the cheek and give them a hug.

Each time, I grip the handrail and creep down in my nightgown to shake their hands and tell a joke or two. "What happened to the woman who had big boobs when she broke the law?" Pause and wait. "She got busted!" I always tell that joke. That is my dad's joke. He told me it would win over the guys and it does. They laugh and hoist me in the air, carry me on their wide shoulders and broad, hairy backs. I creep down and make them laugh or I will be invisible, like those people up in the rooms sleeping, the ones not invited to the party. Invisible is the worst thing to be. Invisible is another word for "not there" and I have been outrunning that feeling for as long as I can remember.

STEWART'S ROOT BEER STAND

We're up at the counter, sitting on circular stools that turn back and forth. I swing myself around and back to the counter, around and back to the counter, around and back to the counter. My dad orders "Two frosty mugs—make sure they're frosty!" of birch beer, two straws, bendy straws. As I drink the birch beer, my teeth chatter and I get a cold headache, but it's the best thing I've ever tasted. My dad puts his hand on my back. "Isn't that good, beautiful? You look so good today."

I'm sitting here with my dad at Stewart's, and it's just the two of us. My dad's in full uniform. His gun is in his holster, his badge up by his chest. I love the way his uniform sparkles, all of the little buttons and brass pins on his lapel. I know everyone in the place is looking at my dad and me. I spin myself around in a circle again, hit my palms on the counter. Spin myself around in a circle one more time, palms on the counter. My dad says, "Ok, ok, cut it out." I can't help myself. I'm so excited. I'm excited to be here with my dad, to be his daughter, sitting here at Stewart's drinking the best birch beer on earth and sitting on the coolest stool, right up at the front of the restaurant. I spin myself around in a circle one more time. My dad grabs my thigh with his big hand. "I said, stop it!" I look down at my thigh. There are five red circles where his fingers dug into my white flesh. I feel them and then I don't. The same people that I felt were watching me and my dad with admiration now turn to look at us again, I feel, in disgust. He touched me on my thigh in front of all these people. I wonder if these marks will stay. Why couldn't I have just listened to him? Why couldn't I have kept this visit perfect? I fight back tears and a huge lump forms in my throat. I try to take another sip of my birch beer but nothing moves up the straw. My dad says, "C'mon, finish up. I gotta get outta here. Did you think I could stay here all day?"

CAMEO

for Helen Casale

A fabric made of moths,
my grandmother replenishes
the blouse and petticoats,
sweating under the heat of July.

Everywhere white sheets cling
to banisters. Amidst tins of talc,
boxes of bobby pins, and long red
threads dangling from ornate boxes, she tells

me of her father: immigrant
from Germany, left his family,
everything, pursued
the dream. "Taught me to weld

and solder. To be more than just
a girl." Beads of sweat line her faint
mustache. I am lulled by her rhythmic
wheeze of three packs

a day for over 40 years, the burning
air surrounding her. I
count the multicolored heads
of pins leaping from

the tomato pin cushion as
I nibble her fresh Queen Anne's lace
cookie, powdered sugar falling
on the wooden floor in a reverse

cameo. My grandmother
hems the crepe and chiffon, her
fingers buzzing with
the work of women.

PERFECT

I remember my brother, one year old, as a beautiful baby doll propped against the aluminum siding of our house, on top of our backyard steps, all shiny, hair soft, face slack, with beautiful brown eyes, deep set, lips parted, staring. This moment stopped time. I'm four years and 10 months old and I love him like I've never loved anyone. I can actually feel my heart getting bigger in my chest. I want him to stay out of time. I want him to never get any bigger, my little doll baby boy. I want to hold him, swallow him whole, lock him in my heart, wrap him in ribbon, put him in my pocket—some golden ember, light and hot, glowing for me. Perfect, perfect, he is so perfect.

Perfect... I'm your perfect little girl, Daddy's little angel girl, your baby doll, you called me baby. *You're my baby.* When you hold me in your arms I dissolve into you, and when you hold me in your arms, with those big hands... those big hands.

BEATEN PATH

For my brother, there were slappings across the face and beatings with belts, being punched and thrown out of moving cars. Our father was constantly at him and it was my job to protect him from it. I had an "in" with our dad and was able to talk him down off the ledge he seemed so often to stand on.

When I was little and dad worked in a jail as a security officer, he would come home late and angry; the only thing that could soothe him was me. I would approach him like he was a wounded animal. Soon—at three years old I knew this—I would gauge the slow climb up onto his lap and then hug him. Eventually, he'd relax into my hug. Sometimes he would cry, and I knew I carried a power, one that, as I got older, I'd often need to keep him calm. The worst thing that could happen to me was hearing my brother scream, being beaten by my father while I was downstairs, pulling the pillow over my head, trying to drown out the sound, knowing I had failed.

Once, I forged my father's signature on my brother's report card so that he wouldn't see it; of course, he found out. My father brought me upstairs to discipline me and made me take down my pants. He removed his belt as I sat on the end of the bed, and said, "Do you know why I am doing this?" I nodded, and then he pulled me, gently almost, onto his lap. And I waited, pants around my ankles and bare-bottomed, for him to beat me with that belt. My body stiffened like a board and I knew there was no way I would allow tears. As the leather cracked against my skin, I knew that I had won.

WAITING AT PENN STATION

May I have your attention please. This is a special announcement for New Jersey Transit passengers waiting to board the Northeastern Corridor train, the scheduled 6:01 Trenton express. This train is being delayed en route from Sunnyside Yard due to signal problems in the East River tunnel. Just as soon as train 3963 has arrived in the station and is ready for boarding, the track number will be posted and announced. New Jersey Transit and Amtrak apologize for this delay. Thank you.

I look over and see my brother standing, hands in the pockets of his jeans, shoulders rounded, watching the board for his track listing. I have an unbelievably strong urge to run my hands through the close crop of his crew cut like I did when we were young, but I have no idea how this will be received so I keep my hands in my jacket pockets and look down at the filthy Penn Station floor. We stand in silence until he asks me, "Do you remember Teddy?"

Yes. How can I ever forget him? The strange man with greasy black hair who worked at my grandfather's gas station. He was related to us only peripherally, through marriage, as his sister was married to my dad's brother. He always seemed to like spending time with children more than adults and took all of us kids to shows and movies and camping trips with our smiling, waving parents' consent. Teddy had a cool blue VW bus with the back seats removed, allowing it to open into an enormous play area with colorful, fake fur-lined walls and a steady stream of kids' music blasting through the speakers. But he scared me and I didn't know why. Maybe it was the way his mouth always seemed to smile without the rest of his face, a kind of smile that never really seemed happy, a wolfish smile filled with bent, yellow teeth and breath that reeked of cigar smoke.

I remember he took me and Chris on a day trip out to Gettysburg to learn firsthand about the Civil War and visit battlefields and monuments. The facts of the day, even fleeting moments of it, are irretrievable to me. The only clear memories I have are the bookends of the drive there and back. While my brother slept on the mattress in the back of the van, I stayed up front with Teddy in the passenger seat. I loved being able to look out the wide windows of the front of the van and see the lights on the road streak by as we passed. After a long silence, Teddy asked, "Wanna drive?"

"I can't... drive," I stammered. Keeping his one hand

on the wheel, Teddy used his other to pull me to him.

"Climb on my lap."

"I... I don't want to crash."

"You won't. I am right here. Now put your hands on the wheel. Good, good. Okay, see you are driving!"

And with that, he removed his hands from the wheel. My mind was getting that fuzzy feeling and I was starting to sweat. I kept my hands firmly on the wheel, eyes on the road.

"Good. Good. You are doing great," Teddy said as his hands slowly lifted the bottom of my shirt and began to stroke the bottom of my belly, then the top of my belly and then... I was starting to feel queasy. His greasy breath in my ear, sandpaper hands on my skin, Teddy said, "Don't let go. We could crash, you know." If I let go, it would be my fault if we crashed. My fault. But I was already crashing... into rocks on the shore as the waves beat against my skin and rubbed me raw, away from feeling. Away.

"Yes, I remember him." And in a moment I know. I know why my brother has asked me. I stand, just staring at him until finally his eyes meet mine and he nods in a funny way I have never seen him do before. The air seems to have been vacuumed out of Penn Station. No, not Chris. I am glued to the spot. I can't move. I feel sick. Someone runs the wheel of their luggage over my feet as they sprint for their train. Suddenly, his train is called and Chris hugs me and goes.

When I finally am able to walk, my mind thrusts itself into overdrive. I find myself cocking my head to the side as I walk, desperate for more memories, more evidence. Why can't I remember more? I want to remember. Our Pennsylvania trip... during a day off... what happened? Everything is grainy and out of focus and... gone. All that comes to me are flashes of three photographs taken the day of that trip:

Snapshot 1: I am straddling a military tank wearing a red mock turtleneck, red pants, and a short boyish haircut. Behind me is my brother, still climbing the tank, on all fours, face looking down at its metal surface. I smile at the camera with a green and red striped candy straw between my teeth. But I am not the focus of the picture. The camera is aimed squarely at my brother's downward turned body.

Snapshot 2: Chris wearing Teddy's favorite cowboy hat, almost dwarfing his head. My brother is wearing his favorite t-shirt while it is still in relatively good condition and sucking on a brown candy straw.

Snapshot 3: a picture of my brother taken from behind. He is looking over his shoulder at the camera with a face that says he is unprepared for the picture.

Something about these pictures has always felt wrong to me. I could never understand why. But for as long as I could remember, holding them seemed to blur my vision, pushing me to look past the photographs into something I couldn't see.

I snap back to Penn Station and find I have to lean against the storefront of a Dunkin' Donuts so as not to fall over. I rest my full weight against the smooth tiles there and slide slowly to the floor. I now know why I could never look at those photos without my heart lurching. Everything blurry is now in focus. The darkened room I had so often entered, fumbling and desperate for my bearings, has suddenly been plunged into light. My baby brother. I was meant to protect him. How didn't I see? For a terrifying moment, I know exactly how my mother must feel.

"Hey, you can't sit here," a Penn Station police officer calls to me.

But where can I go from here? I hear myself say, "Okay, I'm leaving." I slowly pick myself up off the floor and walk toward the exit sign marked Seventh Avenue, up the escalator and out into the pouring rain. I have no umbrella, but it doesn't matter now. I can only think one thought over and over again. I failed my brother and I need to make it right. But how? And the answer comes to me so clear, like someone else's voice echoing in my head, "Kill Teddy. Buy a gun, find him and kill him."

MEETING

I'm nervous... my name is Terri and... shit. I know what I am supposed to say next. This is my first meeting and still I know. I mean, I've seen it in movies for Christ's sake. That's why I didn't want to come here today. I feel like a fucking cliché.

It's just that I don't know if I am an alcoholic or not... I mean, my life sucks. I know that much. I know my drugs are out of control and that thing about your life being unmanageable, well, that is definitely true for me, too. It's just that this feels like a much bigger thing than just the drinks and drugs. I've felt this way for so long. A long time before I ever drank. I feel like I am disappearing, like my body is made out of sand and I am being slowly funneled down the giant hourglass in the Wizard of Oz, you know, like only my outline is left and it is walking around like a ghost, looking for the rest of me.

I think I came here because I thought maybe you all could help me find the rest. I need to find the rest of me.

8 HULL DRIVE

I love my grandmother Helen and she loves me. She lets me sleep overnight at her house on Hull Drive sometimes. I love the white house with black shutters, even though the white has a green mildewed sheen and the black paint is peeling. There is a giant huckleberry tree that arcs over the driveway, dropping huckleberries that make your car sticky with berries and bird crap. Her lawn is brown and the overgrown grass tickles my knees, which I like, even though the neighbors sometimes call to complain. I get lost in the tall grass and never worry about keeping track of time.

I think she loves me because I climb trees like she did when she was a girl. She says I am free and strong and adventurous. When I stay over, my grandmother and I head down to the supermarket and buy packages of chicken hearts and gizzards or chicken livers. She makes them for me with Uncle Ben's rice with lots of butter and salt and it is always a feast. We sit smacking lips together and when I finish, she puts more and more on my plate. The little chicken hearts are so sweet and rubbery in my mouth and sometimes

I hold one between my teeth to see how long I can go before biting down on it. Then she makes me a German chocolate layer cake from scratch or some kind of sugary pie.

When it is time for sleep we crawl into the same tight little bed that smells of ashes and apples. It is such a small space that once grandmother gets into it, she settles in and doesn't make another move for the whole night. She wakes up in the same position she went to sleep in. She tells me I am a crazy sleeper, moving around at night, calling out in my sleep. She calls me the gymnast sleeper because I even slapped her in the head while I was sleeping once. She asks me what I am running from in my sleep—why can't I ever be still?

I love her. She says I am beautiful and smart and strong. She tells me it is good to climb trees and get dirty and catch tadpoles and garter snakes and then—carefully—let them go.

2:06 AM

Son—
you sleep in the new room;
I caress the impossible, the flat
shell of me, as the great moon
of you rises inside
the pool of my eyes.

DEVELOP

'That was the man who murdered your family! I brought him to you to question... to spit on if you wanted. But you forgave him! How could you do that? Why did you forgive him?'

I answered him the truth: 'Forgiveness is all I have to offer.'

Immaculee Ilibagiza

SPAWNING OF THE HORSESHOE CRABS
for Matt

We wake wrapped in a thin membrane
of sleep, your voice full of silver
and water, a glass on the table,
hours away. My head
on your heart, it beats a wild
triangle in autumn

air. In and out, I drift
into last evening: sunset on the
beach, the hungry
sand at our feet, we gently lifted crab
carcasses to the light. The waves deposited
seaweed—so many strips of emerald
on the berm. Wind soon battered
us to the car. Now we lay on quilted
sheets, cool as bones. We caress
the silence—milk love out of idleness,
our bodies—
mist and rain.

BABY

You have been growing
before you were thought
possible.

Smell of saffron and cinnamon,
wet dough and honey—
skin, dust of gold and pollen
fingernails, soft flakes of shell.

Already, I feel your heartbeat
on my lips—

Hurry.

I have made a space
for you between
the lines
of my
palm.

WATCHING HIM GO

I am watching him go. He lifts his unusually large-for-a-4-year-old-body up the steep steps of the school bus. My breath is catching in my throat, at once proud and helpless. I have been steadying myself for this journey since he was born. He seems impossibly young and yet so fully independent. After boarding, he stands at the top step, takes one more brief look back at me, and smiles. I am watching my limb at the top of the bus. He takes his seat in the middle and waves from the window. No, no, no... he cannot be getting on a bus. It's too soon. He's just not ready. An animal-like sound escapes my throat and Freddy the bus driver looks at me with his ear thrust out to catch what I have said. I can't speak so I just wave my hand. He pulls the big lever to the side, the doors shut in front of me, and I stand, stunned. Suddenly, I come to. I realize with alarm that I am still there.

"Oh my God, the car."

I run as fast as wobbly legs will take me to my minivan, where I throw myself into the front seat so violently I bang my thigh against the steering wheel.

Later, I will find a quarter-sized bruise there and wonder how I didn't feel any pain in the moment. The keys still in the ignition, I quickly turn them and begin to drive. I don't have time or the presence of mind to put on my seatbelt. All I know is that I must follow the bus. I am in a cold sweat. I panic. I look in the rearview mirror to glance at the back seat. There is no child sitting in the car seat. My heart stops for a moment, but the immediacy of the situation jump-starts me back into focus.

"Come on, come on… come on."

I am watching the back of the bus. Is my son still seated? Will he stand to look back for me? Is he talking to someone? Is he afraid? Maybe he changed his mind and is crying for the bus driver to turn around and go back for me. Will something bad happen to him on this bus? I suddenly notice that I am rocking back and forth at the wheel and am sweating even more as the panic escalates.

At the opening to the highway, panic in full swing, I realize that I will have to wait my turn at the merge and won't be able to stay directly behind the bus. I strike the steering wheel with the bottom of my palm, over and over as I wait for the bus to merge ahead of me. My brain begins firing off options. Do I risk pulling out quickly with the bus? Is there a shortcut I can take to the school? The bus finds an opening and pulls out ahead of me. I accelerate to the end of the ramp and brake quickly. Cars whoosh by as I anxiously wait for a space to enter. I can see the bus rolling down the highway, away from me.

"Oh, no. I am losing it! No, no, no... please God, no!"

I pull out, cutting off another car. Its horn blares in my ears from behind. I don't care. I have to catch up to the bus. I speed down the highway, down the off ramp and arrive in time to watch the bus make a wide turn into the circle in front of the school. I follow directly behind it until I am waved with a friendly smile towards the side lot. I am not allowed to park in the circle behind the bus. They want me to park to the right of the school.

"Shit, shit, shit," I mutter under my breath and pound the steering wheel. I am biting my nails and circling the lot in full-blown panic mode until I finally find a spot. I park on a crazy angle with slightly enough room to open my door and squeeze out. Barely having thrown the car into park and turned the engine off, I leap out of the car, leaving the keys in the ignition. I don't care. Steal the van, for fuck's sake. I need to find my son. I scan the circle for him. Lines and lines of children are being directed into the school, but which bus is his? Where is he? I am playing the Where's Waldo game, hoping to spot my son's flaming red hair in the organized chaos of the crowd.

"There!" I yell, making the person next to me jump and suck her teeth. I push past two people just in time to catch a glimpse of him parading into school in a line.

"Rainer! Look over here! It's mommy!"

He scans the air towards my voice, searching for my face as I jump up in the air and wave.

My son waves gently and peacefully back, his backpack like a large animal holding onto his tiny shoulders. I watch him walk into the building, smiling and waving until at last his outline disappears into the large waiting school. When he is completely out of sight, my knees buckle and I fall onto the curb. I put my head in my hands and start to cry.

BLANK DAY

Scraped clean
by the sounds beneath
her, his body
hissed like water
into an empty space
as she opened
against the will
of her heel
dug sharply into
the dip of
the gray mattress.

Before he was in
her as white as white
above white
her veins dark as
bruises, he carefully removed
his shoes, folded and draped
his shirt then
his pants over
the bedpost, marking
where he'd been.

FUNERAL

You push me from the inside
you're clawing to get out.

You're tearing my insides
with your big hands.

Your big hands—
that finger missing the tip

from the war—the war
where you killed that girl and raped the other one—

lost yourself. I remember the finger, that finger
how I could tell it was you

in the casket.
In the casket you seemed

to smile at me—
I knew you'd come back—

you'd never leave me alone
leave me alone—

I dream about you while I sleep
I dream about you while I walk

and work and think and fuck and act and
create and try just try to have a life without you

without you. I wish I could live without you.

I feel you kick at me

I'm losing you.
I'm afraid. I want
to break this

before you push into me
hook your finger into me

pry me open
I'm so tight

you pry me
open, scrape me out

of me, crack
my shell blue as the sea

you find the hidden
meat of me

fish your tongue inside
of me, suck the tender me from me

till I am empty—
sun-warmed, hollow.

PERFECT #2

Perfect little girl... little girl, little, little me under the weight of big, big you. Daddy, you sing, you hold my face, I'm eclipsed by you. You've pinned me down—one arm held by your head and shoulder, the arm, my other arm held by your big, big hand. Held out like I'm being crucified. You sing our song, *Closer... let me whisper in your ear... say the words you long to hear. I'm in love with you...* You pin my legs with your legs. You slide your hand down my stomach. *Listen, do you want to know a secret?* Do you want to know a secret? Perfect little girl, so smart. She knows just when to say... nothing.

THE BAR

Hey. Look at me. *Look* at me. Come on, I'll let you look at me. Yeah you, black leather pants. Or you... who cares? Buy me a drink, man. I'm itchy tonight. I need something indefinable. I could define it in you, if you like. Come over here and kiss me. Fuckin' kiss me or something! Bartender, give me another one, will ya? Long Island Iced Tea and a tequila shot. I need to loosen up. I'm tight in all the wrong places.

Tonight was supposed to be easy, here on Avenue A. Pyramid Club, some club—it's just a bar, man... it's a fuckin'... Yeah, I'm sitting on the fuckin' bar! You have a problem with that? Fuck these people! My goddamned fishnets are riding up my ass. I wish I wore my other boots. These are killing my feet. Where is my lipstick? Don't tell me I left it at home. I'm like naked up here. And I'm going to college in another month. What's up with that?

Come on... come on look at me... brown leather jacket... quarter to one in the morning... Hey, sideburns, look at me you motherfucker! Hey, green vintage shirt, can't you see I'm dying up here? I need something, anything... you.

IF/LITANY #2

If I walk on the opposite side of the street it will stop;
if I find a shortcut home it will stop; if I count every
mailbox on my way to school; if I pray; if I pray really
hard; if I whisper pleas to the fairies that visit me at
night, the ones that shimmer at the edge of my bed
with airy voices; if I thank them, praise them, love
them more it will stop; if I'm good; if I'm sorry; if I
pray; yes, if I'm good, then it'll stop; if I get straight
A's; if I flunk everything and call attention to myself;
if I wear a lot of makeup and act grown up it will
stop; if I am not a little girl; if I wear no makeup at all
and look tired and sad; if I wear loose and baggy
clothes; if I dress like a little girl; if I dress grown up,
like a woman, with heels and a low cut shirt, then it'll
stop; if I eat all this food; if I gain so much weight the
pounds will sit on me like armor; if I starve myself
and only eat one piece of celery it will stop; if I starve
myself till I am bones and then under my white
porous ribs—beneath it all when there is nothing left
to lose and I am invisible—then it will stop; if I weigh
myself 100 times a day; if I line up the papers on the
desk absolutely perfectly; if one of the edges of the
octagonal glass is placed perfectly in line with one of

the ridges in the table; if I drive far, fast in my car; if I ride on the back of a motorcycle without a helmet, traveling the backroads of some small town in the middle of Nowheresville America with someone I barely know, traveling so fast, gulping the hard burning air, feeling the wind pound me out of myself into someone new, someone I don't recognize, someone with no past and no future, just a now where anything can happen, then it will stop; if I seduce danger, chase adrenaline down the tiny streets of a foreign city; if I drive drunk, jump from steep cliff walls into the freezing lake below, ride on the roof of a car while it is speeding down the street, run across the train tracks to see if I can beat the train, antagonize some drunk person until they want or need to hit me, beat me, hurt me, feel my nose pop as radius of knuckle cracks slope of bone, then it will stop; if I take all these drugs; if I don't take any; if I take all these drugs; if I drink myself into oblivion; if I mix drinking and drugs; if I drink and drink and drink and drink; if I take a new drug and then another; if I take it in a new place; if I take it and dance against the will of my exhaustion, then it will—if I sleep with a thousand men; if I stop sleeping with anyone; if I don't sleep with men; if I sleep with women, then it'll stop; if I don't sleep at all at night; if I keep myself awake as long as I can; if I only sleep two hours a night; if I run my wrist under the hottest water possible, holding it there until what once felt hot along my wrist runs cold over my body; if I get the razor blade out and slowly drag it along my skin, once and then again, watching as the tiniest droplets of blood form; if I can push myself to go deeper, to keep tracing the same line with the razor; if I cut and cut to a place so numb that I stop feeling the razor; if I cut and cut and cut deeper into that numbness, into some place so deep inside, a place I have tried to reach before in so many other ways but never could, it was just too far, so far it would snake down in between the shattered pieces, inside the inlets, the fjords, the tiny fissures and cracks left in me; if—if—if I could only go there, could finally cut, or drug, fuck, drink, adrenalize, perfect my way into the pinprick place of stillness somewhere inside of me—

then... it will finally stop.

ON THE COUCH

It's come to this. Lying on a couch in a quiet room under a painting by Van Gogh, a field of flowers, talking to this woman.

Beneath my body the couch, cool green fabric on my skin, it's grass, I tell myself. I try to feel the grass, smell the grass, touch the grass... God, I wish I still smoked grass... is so tall. My body sinks into it, leaving my outline, a snow angel in the grass, can you make grass angels? My small frame... my small frame is... no.... Back to the ceiling is high and white hot light in my eyes. It's the sun, yes the sun. I lie back and I am there.

Up at the surface, the Woman in the Quiet Room with the Van Gogh painting and the green couch is calling me. She wants to lead me back somewhere— the grass, focus on the grass... remember, the grass is so tall she can't find you. But she's digging into my dirt. There's something under, something deeper, breathe—she's covering me in the dirt—breathe— I'm suffocating under the weight of each new shovel of dirt—breathe—there's no air and I must get up from the grass to breathe...

It's the couch, we're on the couch in the living room
under the big windows—on the wall hangs a painting
of flowers in a field—my father has me trapped under
the weight of him—trapped so that I cannot
breathe—breathe—so I turn myself into the rag doll
in the flip book from second grade. I'm jumping rope,
frame by frame by frame his frame my frame is his
frame hovers. It blocks out the sun. The shimmering
light of the day in the grass stops. There is no light.
Just a shadow of my father stretched longer and
longer—

He reaches down to pick me up, a doll in his big
hands.

BACK TO THE OLD HOUSE

I need some old documents, so I return. Once inside, it seems as though the house is melting. The wooden eaves droop and the gray porch lists to the left of the baseboards being swallowed by broken cement. I stand rooted. I know in my bones what is inside. Clutter and filth. Moldy books stacked as high as can be, balanced on a cat urine-scented carpet, three old fish terrariums leaning against one another, their filters and stones inside, dusty and dry, fifty green garbage bags filled with old clothing and blankets, thirty plants spilling over shelves and boxes—boxes everywhere.

Familiar sensations: the spreading warmth in my limbs, dry mouth, jelly-legs and rapid heartbeat. I just stand, allowing them to make their way through me again. The house is coming for me. Finally, it wants to engulf and bury me. I stifle my gag reflex and will myself upstairs. I have to get what I came for.

BONES

I sit in the stillness of a therapist's office, coaxing stray elements of memory into my hand. Some days we catch smoke—the dark x-ray sheet of my mind becomes, for a moment, illumined by the gentle backlight of her prompting. Then—I am inverted, clawing to hold the edges of the now. The room becomes white and bare and stripped of everything that made it feel like mine.

Sometimes the trance of falling into time is euphoric, lightweight, dreamlike and beautiful. Everything glows, glistening water over stones and space has delicate frosted edges and intimate soft pulsating lights. Rubberbanded out of yourself, the way the weightlessness of water relieves unforgiving joints.

But most times, you are gone and it is different. Limbs get heavier and heavier until they become dead things by your side. Nausea and itchiness—beetles crawling under your skin, tumbling in and out of movie frames, the sticky displacement from time— opening mouths quiver and no words come. A great bellowing inside, but the words are stuck, safety pins swallowed that suddenly open into the purple aperture of throat.

I do my best not to fall into the rabbit hole. I avoid every situation that might bring disjointed time—the odd word or phrase, too much stress on a syllable, the way an S trails off the end of someone's tongue when they talk. Or it could be getting up too suddenly after lying down, any flashing lights, the smell of certain trees in spring, the feel of something soft and gelatinous in my mouth or overwhelming exhaustion after having to stay awake. At first, you don't know what will make it come. Soon, you come to expect and wait for it. You know it will come, like a child knows when the bully has touched feet on the playground. Your bones know.

BACKYARD PATIENT

Monarch sutures zucchini
blossoms to the waiting air—
thorax stitching carbon
to slate, pool,

cloud, me. Proboscis extracts
tumor. Breathe in
and out.
Again,

in. Out.
Forewing studies ribs. My belly—
a pop-eyed frog croak.
Tomato plants slice

air into yellow, the rings
on my nails—segmenting
an oak. Below my feet,
dinosaurs impregnate the earth.

HUNGRY

A steel-blue storm outside—I want you
to come home. Mason jars catch
rainwater from rushing
gutter pipes, my black ink bleeds

into paper. For ten years, your breath
has eased its way into
my lungs. I imagine our legs,
vines reaching, toes open as

petals. Or tonight it could be
a delicate press against
the scalloped edge of my satin
slip. How soft is

the landscape of
possibility? The clock neglects
me. The electric hum of
telephone poles outside. I tap

the egg on the waiting
pan. Translucent cold stings my
fingers. Every instant without
your touch, the poverty

of my hands. I sit inside
the pooling hours.

CHRISTMAS EVE, 1979
for Chris

Crushed gravel in our
driveway, where we stepped,
black pushed through

the glow under our feet. Against
my tattered coat, my heart
beat a clear, strong signal:

tonight we are safe. Soon, fat
flakes on my brother's
cheek settled for an

instant and melted
into his moistened
face. Some suspended

in our eyelashes, cut
the light into fractions,
breaching the

lamppost, the street. Our
street. Under the shadows
of leafless branches, the night

rang out, a gong
through the midnight air.

RIALTO BEACH

for Rainer and Atticus

We walk the mist across broken
shells whose inhabitants still cling
to pearly walls, wet hearts out
of casings, edges softened

like memories with the rubbing
of time. Spread across the gray
expanse, mammoth bodies
of red timber take shape—

an eagle talon, a chiseled face,
walking closer, the wide mouth
of a lion, until we stand right in front
of what is simply a felled

tree, shape-shifting the way
time loses its arc—
toes gripping sand.
Our almost two year-old

draws long lines in the shore with a stick
as our older son sings to the sea-stacks,
teetering on the edge of still
more driftwood—shifting

into something wordless
as the tide begins to rush in,
erasing our every footstep,
and the wind and waves beat—

beat, beat on like the infinite.

EPILOGUE: FINISH LINE

The horn goes off. 1,000 feet pound the boardwalk across the starting line. Sunken Meadow 5K along the shore of the Long Island Sound. The rhythm of pounding shoes, of hundreds of people breathing, creates meditation. I try to pace myself. I know I can't start out too fast or I might not finish. I start to measure my breathing. Open fish mouth, jaw loose, make sure the air comes in and out, lean slightly forward, let the breath fall into a rhythm, into the rhythm of pounding feet. I have to run and I have to finish. It feels right. The slicing air in my lungs and the tightness in my calves feel full of purpose, and vital. I am running. I have to run. I've always been running.

One mile split, 8:44, remember that, 8:44, not bad. Are you going too fast? Are you going to be able to finish? Nagging doubts. Strangely, it is my father's voice that comes to me, saying *You can do it. You can finish.* His voice is both the doubt and the propulsion. *You can do anything you want to do, my strong, beautiful girl, and no one will ever love you like me.*

I know my body is strong. The 38 hour labor and how much this body has held. We're all running. The older man next to me leans to one side as he runs, gasping asthmatically; he sounds terrible. Like he's not going to make it. I wish I could carry him on my back and, again, I think of my father, a small boy watching his mom bring in the men, one after another for rent money, until raising three boys was just too much. Foster care, orphanages and monthly visits. How far he had to run. How much he carried and what he lay down at my feet.

17:15. Second mile. Okay, two-thirds there. No giving in now. My father is back and his voice is so fucking clear. He is right next to me and when I see him, he is young and running in fatigues on a foreign beach and his face is red with sunburn and he is scared but yells into my face anyway. *You shut up and just do it. You finish. You make me proud. If you want something, you go and take it. Only the strong make it. You take what you need and you beat them, beat them all and run and win and...* No, that isn't how I want to finish. That isn't the fuel I need anymore. I am not racing against anyone but me this time. I turn to my side and no one is next to me. I am running the last leg alone.

Then, I see it. The finish line. I am almost there. I squint for the time. How am I doing? It doesn't matter now. I will finish. I am running and I will finish. The race is almost over. I am almost there. I dig down for my last reserves. I tell myself: *Finish strong but finish open. Notice as you cross.* And I do: the bluest water, the air smelling of iodine, the blur of tawny sand and a few clouds sitting like piles of snow in a perfectly open sky. Run now, free. Run towards the line, not away from anything.

THE AUTHOR

Terri Muuss is a poet, writer and performer. Her poetry/prose one-woman show, *Anatomy of a Doll*, received grants from New York Foundation for the Arts and Poets and Writers and was named "Best Theatre: Critics' Pick of the Week" by the *New York Daily News*; it has been performed throughout the US and Canada since 1998. Terri's poetry has appeared in *Bolts of Silk*, *Apercus Quarterly*, *Long Island Quarterly*, *Red River Review*, *JB Stillwater* and *Whispers and Shouts* and her poem "Rialto Beach" won the 2013 Great Neck Poetry Prize. She was also the co-producer and host of the monthly Manhattan poetry series *Poetry at the Pulse* for two years.

As a licensed social worker, Muuss specializes in the use of the arts as a healing mechanism for trauma survivors and teaches a course at Rutgers University to social workers entitled *Youth Development Through the Written Arts*. Terri is also an actor, director, motivational speaker, and life coach who specializes in group work and addiction/abuse counseling. She currently lives on Long Island with her husband, writer Matt Pasca, and her two ginger-haired boys, Rainer and Atticus. *Over Exposed* is her first book.

To contact for readings, keynotes, or performances: www.terrimuuss.com.

THE COVER

Cover art and design by Linda Pasca of *Pen & Paper*
www.penandpaperdesign.com

Cover photograph: First Day of Kindergarten, New
Brunswick, NJ, 1974, taken by Leonard Muuss.

THE FOREWORD

Veronica Golos is the author of *Vocabulary of Silence*
(Red Hen Press, 2011), winner of the 2011 New
Mexico Book Award. Poems from *Vocabulary of Silence*
have been translated into Arabic, Italian, Indonesian
and Spanish.

Golos is also the author of *A Bell Buried Deep*, co-
winner of the Nicholas Roerich Poetry Prize (Story
Line Press), co-editor of the Taos Journal of Poetry &
Art, and the Acquisitions Editor for 3:A Taos Press.

Veronicagolos@yahoo.com
www.veronicagolos.wordpress.com

ACKNOWLEDGMENTS

With gratitude to the following journals/anthologies where some poems have previously appeared, sometimes in slightly different forms:

Whispers and Shouts, An Anthology of Long Island Women Poets: "Comfort Food" and "Baby"
Bolts of Silk: "Elkins, NH"
Apercus Quarterly: "Prologue: Panorama" (originally published as "Under the Surface")
Long Island Quarterly: "The Shoe"
Red River Review: "Cameo" (originally published as "The Seamstress")
JB Stillwater Magazine: "Passing" (originally published as "Transience")
Also, *poetryvlog.com* features audio and text of "Scarlet Letter", "T-Shirt", "The Shoe", "Funeral", "Comfort Food" and "Hungry" (posted as "In the Waiting")

Some of the prose pieces appeared in slightly different form in the one-woman show, *Anatomy of Doll*, which opened in NYC at the Abingdon Theatre on September 9th, 1998 with original direction/production by Bernice Rohert/Aulis Theatre Collective.

THANKS

To my miraculous husband, Matt Pasca, and two beautiful boys, Rainer and Atticus: Every story deserves a happy ending. You three are mine. This book, these words, are only made possible by the love I feel from each of you, every day.

To Veronica Golos, friend, sister, mentor, advocate, editor: 18 years from the tiny table at the Trinity apartment to the phone sessions hundreds of miles apart—you have been with my work from the very beginning. I couldn't have envisioned a better editor for this manuscript. Your ear, your vision, the way you lean into the work, your understanding of the words under the words, your beautiful foreword— for all that and more, I profoundly thank you.

To my brother, Chris: We made it. Happiness is possible. Your story/book is next.

To my mother, Helen: We have forged so many new paths together. Whatever you wished to give me when I was little, you have more than delivered to my boys as a grandma. I am so thankful to have you in my life and in theirs.

To Lucretia Anderson, Dave Dopko, Susan Fisher, Ron Gloff, Jewell Handy, Leslie Gurowitz Harris, Liz Howell, Rachel Kaufman, Vernon Larsen, Amy and Ty Lemerande, Serafina Martino and Athena Reich: My profound gratitude for your constant love, friendship and support over these many years.

To Julianne Davis, Danielle Joseph-McKay, and Jennifer Held (my mommy posse): For solidarity, friendship, advice and laughter. And for always accepting me "as is."

To Robyn Kopet: I truly believe you saved my life. Your insight rests on every page. For your extremely sliding scale, never kicking me out, never suggesting medication and always pushing me onward, I thank you.

To my second mom, Harriet: For your spiritual guidance, unwavering support, and unconditional love.

To Linda Pasca: For your amazing work on the cover and for being an inspiration to so many.

To Mary Greaney: I wrote pieces in my head many times while we ran those early mornings. Thanks for always listening during the "dysfunctional family" mile.

To Holly Logue and Jim Murphy: My writing has a theatrical voice you both helped me cultivate during my time in the Kean Theatre Department. Thanks for your guidance. Jim, you are missed.

To Lisa Giacoia: You will never know how much your support of and belief in me has meant.

I asked some of my favorite poets for a "back of the book blurb" and to my delight they said yes. Thank you to Roger Bonair-Agard, Regie Cabico, Deborah Hauser and George Wallace.

To Sonia Bonilla, Nicole Galante and Christina Picardi: For your helpful feedback while the manuscript was in its nascent stages.

To Janet and Art Brennan of JB Stillwater Publishing:

My profound gratitude for this opportunity to share my work with a wider audience. Your overwhelming support of and trust in your writers sets you apart.

And lastly, to every person who has watched my show, listened to me read, asked me to speak or perform at an event, read my work, encouraged me to write, and/or simply believed in me, I humbly thank you.

NOTES

Epigraph: from Rainer Maria Rilke's "The Ninth Elegy", *The Essential Rilke*, translated by Galway Kinnell and Hannah Liebmann (Ecco, revised edition, 2000).

SHUTTER epigraph: from Veronica Golos' poem "The Warrior", *Vocabulary of Silence* (Red Hen Press, 2011).

Flashback: Corner of 183rd Street: references the song "Sweet Dreams (Are Made of This)", written and performed by the British pop duo Eurythmics (Annie Lennox and David A. Stewart) and released in 1983 as their album's title track.

Scarlet Letter: title taken from the 1850 work of fiction of the same name, written by Nathaniel Hawthorne.

FOCUS epigraph: from Brian Turner's "The Hurt Locker", *Here, Bullet* (Alice James Books, 2005).

Between the Dark and the Daylight: title taken from the first line of "The Children's Hour" by Henry Wadsworth Longfellow.

CLICK epigraph: from Sharon Olds' poem "I Go Back to May 1937", *Strike Sparks: Selected Poems 1980-2002* (Alfred A. Knopf, 2004).

DEVELOP epigraph: from pg. 204 of the memoir *Left to Tell: Discovering God Amidst the Rwandan Holocaust* by Immaculee Ilibagiza with Steve Erwin (Hay House, 2007).

Perfect #2: references the song "Do You Want to Know a Secret" by the Beatles, from their 1963 album *Please Please Me*, sung by George Harrison, written by Lennon/McCartney.

Rialto Beach: part of Olympic National Park in Washington State.

Back to the Old House: title references the song of the same name from the album *Hatful of Hollow* by the English rock band The Smiths, released in November, 1984.

Other Releases from JB Stillwater

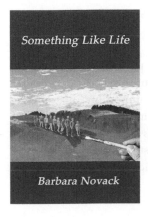

Something Like Life
Barbara Novack
ISBN: 9781937240097
Genre: Poetry

In this neat and intelligent book of poetry "Something Like Life" author Barbara Novack describes the often subliminal messages that are sent to us every day in the beauty and sadness we often see around us in nature and human experience.

Orphan Thorns
Lynn Strongin
ISBN 9781937240066
Genre: Poetry

In this touching and often heart wrenching book, Lynn Strongin explores the beauty of the human soul and its ability to rise above physical as well as psychological illness.

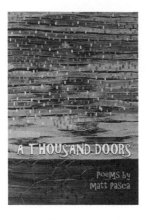

A Thousand Doors
Matt Pasca
ISBN: 9780984568161
Genre: Poetry

Pasca's work pays homage to Kisa Gotami's quest to save her son by finding a home where, impossibly, no suffering has befallen the inhabitants. In the end, A Thousand Doors testifies to the necessity of sharing our stories with courage and vulnerability, and how doing so can lead us further down the path of joy.

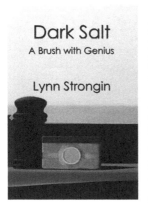

Dark Salt: A Brush with Genius
Lynn Strongin
ISBN: 9780984568147
Genre: Poetry

In this collection of late works by Lynn Strongin, we find that perfect balance of salt and water spiced with symbolism and metaphor that poet Strongin does so well. Jewish Temple offerings included salt and Jewish people still dip their bread in salt on the Sabbath as a remembrance of those sacrifices.

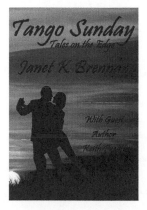

Tango Sunday
Janet K. Brennan
ISBN: 9781937240165
Genre: Short Stories

"Tango Sunday" is a collection of fictional short stories about life on the edge. In Janet Brennan's seventh book, she never fails to seduce the reader into realizing that life is not always as it seems to be. True to Janet Brennan's style and philosophy, she titillates the ready with good doses of revenge, ghosties, life in the spiritual world and death. Author Brennan aptly demonstrates in these dark and twilight zone tales that "Life simply is."

Echoes of My Soul
Lisa Arnold
ISBN: 9781937240172
Genre: Poetry

"Echoes of My Soul" is a powerful collection of poems from emerging poet Lisa Arnold. Lisa's boldly written and vividly expressed poems explore faith, spirituality, fear, death, hope and redemption. The poems included in this captivating book are heart-wrenching and spiritually uplifting as well as fearlessly bold and intense. "Echoes of My Soul" is a striking debut from a gifted and prolific poet that takes readers on a journey and allows readers to peek inside one woman's heart and soul.

Weather Vanes

Summer separates our (bodies)
 in the sweaty nights
(Yet) (till) we ~~reach~~ across the distance
   reach
    to keep in touch
(Though) we still reach across the distance
(Yet) to keep in touch.

→ Autumnal chill/draws our bodies close/
  we take turns
Autumnal chill (Closes windows)
    draws our bodies close.
  We take turns playing host
    to each other's (body.)

Winter finds us seeking warmth
~~(against) puts~~ in one another's skin
~~(in) each other's (skin)~~
Arms & legs embracing ~~our~~ bodies
~~and~~ we hold (~~each other~~) (tight.)

We restore our balance
  when we let the springtime (in)
you trust me & I trust you
  play tag through the (night)

Weather Vanes

Summer separates our bodies
    on the sweaty nights,
Yet we still reach across the distance
    to keep in touch.

Autumnal chill ~~closes~~ shuts the (windows)
~~and it makes us draw~~ close.
We take turns playing host
    to each other's body.

Autumnal chill draws us close,
    We shut (the) windows ~~and~~ & take turns
playing host to each other's body.

~~Autumnal chill draws us close.~~
~~We shut the windows~~
~~And take turns playing host~~
~~to each other's body.~~

Autumnal chill shuts the windows,
    Drawing close (we take turns)
~~We take turns~~ playing host
    to each other's body.

Hymn Weathervanes **Season Suite** Seasonal Hymn

Summer kept [~~us our bodies~~] us / at a distance
3 as we slept (in the steamy/sweaty nights
Still we reached through the pain between us
~~when we wanted to~~ to keep in touch lost
when we

Right ~~on cue~~, ~~the~~ the autumnal chill
drew ~~our~~ our bodies close lost
2 why Winter found us seeking warmth   we take turns play host
in the shelter of our skin   to each other body
against each others skin

Spring rested on balance as we
let the
We regained our balance
when we let the springtime in

~~Throwing upon the waters~~ ~~a toast~~ we rested
we rested our balance
our balance
When we let the springtime in.
~~Playing~~ tag throughout the night
~~Touching~~ tighter,
touching
now I touch you &   hymnal thigh
I touch you, & you now touch me.

CPSIA information can be obtained at www.ICGtesting.com
Printed in the USA
LVOW01s1532070913

351438LV00027B/858/P

9 781937 240233